Toward Renewed Economic Growth in Latin America

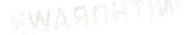

BELA BALASSA

GERARDO M. BUENO

PEDRO-PABLO KUCZYNSKI

MARIO HENRIQUE SIMONSEN

Toward Renewed Economic Growth in Latin America

EL COLEGIO DE MEXICO
FUNDAÇÃO GETÚLIO VARGAS
INSTITUTE FOR INTERNATIONAL ECONOMICS

Mexico City   Rio de Janeiro   Washington, D.C.
1986

Bela Balassa, a Visiting Fellow at the Institute for International Economics, is Professor of Political Economy at the Johns Hopkins University and Consultant to the World Bank.

Gerardo M. Bueno is a Senior Research Fellow at El Colegio de Mexico. He was formerly Director General of the National Council for Science and Technology of Mexico and was Ambassador of Mexico to the European Economic Community and to Belgium and Luxembourg.

Pedro-Pablo Kuczynski is Co-Chairman of the First Boston International Bank in New York and was formerly Minister of Energy and Mines in Peru.

Mario Henrique Simonsen is Director of the Graduate School of Economics at the Fundação Getúlio Vargas. He is a former Minister of Finance and Minister of Planning of Brazil.

INSTITUTE FOR INTERNATIONAL ECONOMICS
11 Dupont Circle, NW
Washington, DC 20036
(202) 328-0583 Telex: 248329 CEIP
C. Fred Bergsten, *Director*
Kathleen A. Lynch, *Director of Publications*
Ann L. Beasley, *Production Coordinator*
Stephen Kraft, *Designer*

The Institute for International Economics was created, and is principally funded, by the German Marshall Fund of the United States.

Library of Congress Cataloging-in-Publications Data
Balassa, Bela A.
Toward renewed economic growth in Latin America.

Bibliography: p. 84
1. Latin America—Economic policy. 2. Latin America—Commercial policy. 3. Finance—Latin America.
4. Latin America—Politics and government—1948
I. Title.
HC125.B22 1986   338.98   86–15253
ISBN 0–88132–045–5

Contents

Preface

The countries of Latin America face a historical turning point. Their present crisis has five dimensions: economic, social, political, institutional, and international. Each offers immense challenges to the peoples and policy makers of the Western Hemisphere, the United States and Canada as well as Latin America itself. Each aspect must be addressed effectively if the crisis is to be resolved.

In *economic* terms, the countries of Latin America must resolve a crucial dilemma. They must find a way to resume self-sustaining growth which provides job opportunities for their rapidly growing populations. Yet they must also restore market creditworthiness through continued timely servicing of their large external debt.

In *social* terms, the present crisis has had devastating effects. Wages and living standards have fallen to levels of ten or twenty years ago in many countries. The new economic policies must have a positive and early social impact. Economic growth and improved distribution of income must go hand in hand.

In *political* terms, the widespread return to democracy must be nourished. This imperative adds enormously to the need for providing stable economic growth and improved income distribution.

Institutional issues are a fourth element of the crisis. The private sector in Latin America—whether small, medium, or large—has been weakened in most countries by the current crisis. Yet the present confluence of economic imperative and political opening seems both to call for, and to permit, a new approach in which entrepreneurial forces are encouraged to provide the jobs and broad-based growth that are needed.

The *international* dimension completes the equation. External events were the proximate source of the Latin American crisis of the early 1980s. A hospitable external environment is essential if

9

the hemisphere is to achieve the economic and political goals here enumerated. Global economic interdependence requires that the industrial countries, particularly the United States, complement new development strategies in Latin America with sustained and supportive policy efforts of their own.

Our three institutions, based in three different parts of the hemisphere, have sponsored this report in an effort to address several aspects of the challenge—particularly its economic, institutional, and international dimensions—and to offer an action program for responding to them. In suggesting these changes, we fully recognize the substantial differences among countries in the region. Indeed, we will illustrate many of our proposals by reference to these differences. But our primary goal is to establish generalizations that can point the way to a coherent strategy for renewing economic growth in all Latin American countries—although the operational details of any such strategy may have to be tailored quite differently in each country.

We also recognize that our proposed program is ambitious. Some of its components have been attempted before and have foundered in the face of entrenched vested interests. Implementation will not be easy.

But we are convinced that the depth and urgency of the crisis require far-reaching new initiatives. We are encouraged by the movement toward reform which is already apparent throughout the hemisphere. Hence, we offer bold proposals in full realization that they will engender controversy, but with firm conviction that they are both essential and feasible.

The report has been written jointly by a team of authors from Latin America and North America, assisted by Dr. Bergsten in preparing the Overview and Recommendations. It has been informed by extensive consultations throughout the hemisphere with leading personalities in the corporate sector, governments, labor organizations, and universities (listed in appendix A). In addition, two meetings to discuss preliminary drafts were held at the Institute for International Economics in Washington to obtain views from both Latin America and North America. The goal of this report is to offer a new growth strategy for Latin America.

The report was commissioned by the Americas Society, Inc., out of the deep concern of its membership for the future of Latin America and relations between the two parts of the hemisphere.

10

We wish to express our thanks for the active engagement of the Society, and particularly the Latin American members of its Chairman's Council, throughout the effort (participating members of the Boards of both groups are listed in appendix B). Funding, about half of which came from Latin America, was provided by a number of individual members of the Chairman's Council, the Rockefeller Brothers Fund, and the Tinker Foundation. The Inter-American Development Bank made possible the translation of the report. The help of all those who have supported this effort is deeply appreciated.

Mario Ojeda
President
El Colegio
de Mexico

Mario Henrique Simonsen
Director, Graduate
School of Economics
Fundação Getúlio
Vargas

C. Fred Bergsten
Director
Institute for
International
Economics

Summary of Conclusions

1. This report proposes a four-part strategy to restore self-sustaining economic growth in Latin America' and simultaneously to enable the continent to cope with its external debt problems. The strategy aims to achieve economic growth in a way that produces a rapid expansion of employment, better distribution of income, and an improvement of social services.

2. Three elements of this strategy require action by the Latin American countries themselves: outward orientation of economic policy, with heavy emphasis on exports and efficient import substitution; raising the savings level and allocating those savings more efficiently among alternative investments; and a sharp reorientation of the role of government in economic life. A critical fourth element is supportive policy by the industrial countries, notably the United States.

3. Outward orientation can achieve both growth and an improvement in the debt situation. It requires:

- adoption and consistent maintenance of competitive exchange rates
- avoidance of excessive import protection
- use of internationally acceptable export incentives.

4. To reach the level and competitiveness of domestic production needed to achieve growth and to improve the debt situation, the countries of Latin America must support outward orientation by significantly expanding the level of savings available from both domestic and external sources (including reversal of capital flight) and substantially improving the efficiency with which those savings are invested. Steps to this end include:

- maintenance of positive (but not excessive) real interest rates

- tax policies that encourage savings rather than consumption

- reduction in budget deficits, which contribute to inflation and "crowding out" of productive private investment

- inducements for renewed inflow of foreign private capital, particularly in nondebt-creating forms, and reversal of capital flight. Specific measures include liberalization of rules governing direct and other foreign equity investment, creation of mutual funds and repatriation funds, and joining the World Bank's new Multilateral Investment Guaranty Agency.

5.   These policy proposals in turn call for sharp changes in the role of the state in Latin American economic life:

- substantial deregulation to encourage and support entre- preneurial forces

- reducing the state's role as a producer of goods and services

- emphasizing instead providing education, health care, and other basic services effectively, and setting the overall framework for economic growth with supportive macro- economic and microeconomic policies.

6.   The United States and other industrial countries must adopt policies that will support the proposed strategy for Latin America by achieving:

- steady economic growth of at least 3 percent annually, to stimulate world trade and thus promote the needed ex- pansion of Latin American export earnings

- renewed trade liberalization, and avoidance of new import restrictions and export subsidies

- further declines in real interest rates through cuts in excessive budget deficits (notably in the United States), reductions in spreads charged by commercial banks for countries with effective adjustment programs, and the creation of new defenses (as through a compensatory facility at the International Monetary Fund) against any future interest rate upswings

- substantial infusions of new funds to Latin America, on the order of $20 billion annually for the next few years, from the private sector and, most importantly in the near term, the World Bank and the Inter-American Development Bank.

Overview and Recommendations

The 1980s have been a "lost decade" for the economies of most Latin American countries. Per capita income is lower today than in 1980 in every nation in Latin America and has fallen by nearly 10 percent for the region as a whole. For the entire continent, average per capita income in 1985 barely exceeded the level of 1975. In some countries, per capita income has returned to the level of the mid-1960s.

The Economic Crisis

Unemployment has soared, surpassing 15 percent of the urban labor force in several countries. Underemployment has risen even more. The poorest groups have suffered particular hardship. Yet population growth continues at nearly 2½ percent per year, requiring the creation of five million new jobs annually simply to keep unemployment from rising further.

At the same time, some of the largest countries in the hemisphere have been buffeted by rapid inflation. The annual rate of price increase reached 1,200 percent in Argentina and 500 percent in Brazil before their recent monetary reforms. Even excluding Bolivia's hyperinflation, inflation has averaged 150 percent in Latin America in recent years and has exceeded 100 percent annually in a half dozen countries—despite continuing recession and rising unemployment.

Virtually every country in the hemisphere also carries a severe burden of external debt. Total Latin American debt approaches $400 billion, of which two-thirds is owed to commercial banks. One-third of Latin America's export earnings are devoted to paying interest on this debt. Net capital inflows have nearly disappeared since 1983. Latin America has thus been experiencing a $30 billion net outward transfer of resources a year—about 5 percent of its combined gross product.

There are, of course, substantial differences among Latin American countries. Colombia, alone among the major countries, did not borrow excessively in the 1970s and has not needed a debt rescheduling. Ecuador undertook far-reaching reforms but has subsequently suffered the effects of a precipitous fall in oil prices.

The most important exception to many of the generalizations made above, and elsewhere in this study, is Brazil. In 1985–86, Brazil appears to have resumed a substantial degree of self-sustaining growth while continuing to service its large external debt. In 1985, the country grew by more than 8 percent and ran a trade surplus of over $12 billion; similar results seem likely for 1986.

Brazil accounts for over one-third of the population, and of the gross economic product, of the entire region. Hence its progress has profound importance for our overall topic—both in evaluating the policies applied and, perhaps, in offering indications for what can be done elsewhere.

To be sure, Brazil has not solved all its problems. Success is not yet assured for its far reaching monetary reform (the "Cruzado Plan"), adopted in response to its principal immediate problem of inflation. Neither has it adequately improved the distribution of the fruits of its economic growth to the population at large. Most important from the perspective of this report, Brazil's achievements do not obviate the depth of the problems faced by the rest of Latin America.

The Causes of the Crisis

The proximate cause of the economic crisis in Latin America was the global recession of the early 1980s. The combination of steep declines in both the volume and prices of their exports and sharp rises in real interest rates pushed Latin America's external balances into deep deficit. Just when most needed, capital inflows—from both commercial banks and foreign direct investment—fell sharply.

Virtually every country in the region, sooner or later, sought to respond to the crisis by adjusting its domestic economy. Radical alternatives were rejected, except in Peru after 1984. But austerity was required. Initially, imports fell dramatically—by one-third in the region as a whole, by two-thirds in Mexico. Growth was stifled. Unemployment rose and real incomes fell.

Subsequently, some of the countries aggressively promoted exports and began their recovery. But success has been mixed: dramatic progress in Brazil, as noted; an encouraging resumption of growth in Colombia; continuing difficulties in Peru and some smaller commodity exporters; and renewed crisis in Mexico, formerly the most effective adjuster, in large part as a result of the plunge in oil prices in early 1986.

The most profound revelation of the debt crisis, however, was that Latin America faces much deeper economic problems. The global recession and its aftermath exposed the vulnerability of the continent, but the roots of that vulnerability are much more far-reaching. There are three major reasons for this conclusion.

First, many other developing countries were hit at least as hard as Latin America by global recession—yet recovered far more rapidly and far more extensively. The most successful adjusters were the newly industrializing countries (NICs) of East and Southeast Asia, where dependence on world markets is much greater than in Latin America but less reliance was based on foreign borrowing. But some other developing countries, such as Turkey, also recouped rapidly. The only other region that has suffered as long and as much is Africa, which has deep structural problems as well as a much lower level of development, and has been in economic decline since the early 1970s.

Second, Latin America has been experiencing a long-term deterioration in its economic position relative to many other developing countries, and even relative to many industrial countries. The extreme case is Argentina, whose per capita income approached the French level in 1929 but is one-fifth of that today. As shown in chapter 1, however, all of the Latin American countries considered in detail in this report (Argentina, Brazil, Chile, Colombia, Ecuador, Mexico, Peru, Uruguay, and Venezuela) had much higher per capita incomes in 1950 than Korea and Taiwan. Venezuela, Uruguay, and Argentina were ahead of Finland, Austria, and Italy. Chile was ahead of, and Mexico was close to, Spain. Most of the Latin American countries surpassed Greece, Portugal, and Turkey. As late as 1960, several of these countries were ahead of, or roughly equal to, Japan (table 1.2).*

Many of these relative economic positions have changed dramatically over the last generation—a very short period for such historical swings. Average per capita income in the nine Latin American countries is now one-third or less that of Japan and the middle-income European countries, one-half that of Mediterranean Europe, and below that of the Asian NICs and Turkey. From 1950 to 1985, per capita income in all these countries more than tripled—while only Brazil approached such a record in Latin America and the rest of the region lagged substantially. The same story emerges from comparing growth of all exports, exports of manufactured goods (table 1.3), and other economic indices. There can be no doubt that Latin America has fallen dramatically behind Europe and East Asia.

Third, Latin America faced serious economic problems even before the debt crisis broke. Substantial capital flight had already reflected a loss of confidence in some countries of the region. The large external borrowings of the 1970s were not used effectively in many countries, thus failing to create the needed debt-servicing capacity (table 1.5). Unemployment and underemployment were already high in some countries. Rapid inflation emerged periodically. Income maldistribution was widespread. The crisis exposed and intensified these difficulties, but many of them were already present—and, in some quarters, recognized.

The sources of Latin America's fundamental problems are analyzed in the individual chapters of this report. Three sources emerge as most important:

- the inward orientation apparent in most countries, especially in their willingness to let currencies become overvalued (table 2.1) and trade policies to remain protectionist (or become even more so)
- the lack of needed incentives to savings and efficient investment of savings (table 3.1), both domestic and foreign
- the excessive, even suffocating, role of the state [including state enterprises (tables 4.1 and 4.3)] and the concomitant weakening of the private sector.

---

* *Selected tables are presented beginning on page 44.*

Major changes are needed in each of these areas if Latin America is to meet its present and prospective economic challenges. Our recommendations, summarized below, are developed in the supporting chapters.

The Potential of Latin America

Before presenting the proposed strategy, Latin America's potential for addressing its problems constructively must be assessed. The difficulties discussed are substantial. Many are of long-standing duration. Many have grown much worse in the first half of the 1980s. But we believe that Latin America can meet the challenge successfully for a number of reasons.

First is the enormous potential of the continent, in both human and material terms (table 4.5). Its people have demonstrated considerable entrepreneurial abilities, despite government policies that often discourage their realization. Educational levels are relatively high in many countries.

In material terms, Brazil is the world's eighth largest economy. Mexico and Argentina rank in the top 20. Natural resource endowments—especially arable land, oil and mineral reserves, and hydroelectric power potential—are substantial. The industrial base and economic infrastructure are considerable for a "developing" continent.

Second is the actual record of Latin America. Despite its relative decline, already described, economic growth was quite impressive in several Latin American countries following policy reforms in the mid-1960s. And while growth rates declined over the last decade, manufactured exports rose rapidly—especially in countries that promoted exports after the first oil shock in 1973—although none of them matched the export performance of East Asia.

Even in their response to the adversities of the early 1980s, several Latin American countries revealed considerable economic adaptability and political resilience. The region improved its combined current account position by $40 billion from 1981 to 1984, about 6 percent of its gross domestic product. The predicted political instabilities failed to materialize, and democratization proceeded in several countries.

Third, the relatively greater success of other developing countries and regions demonstrates that better results are possible. There is simply no reason to believe that "the Confucian work ethic" or "the Spanish heritage" mean that East Asia can make it while Latin America cannot (chapter 1). In fact, the rapid growth of the "informal sector" in heavily regulated economies, such as Peru, suggests that the problem is not a lack of business acumen but rather an institutional structure that stifles entrepreneurial spirit in these economies. Policies, and the related economic and social structures, matter substantially, as this and many other studies show.

Even leaving East Asia aside, the growing number of "success stories" in the developing world—many in previously improbable locales—cannot fail to both provide a lesson for Latin America and offer hope for its future. Turkey, the "sick man of Europe" for a century or more, may be the first true "graduate" of the debt crisis with its remarkable turnaround since 1980 as it oriented its policies outward. India, whose economy had suffered from intensive governmental regulation, has recorded steady growth throughout this decade—in the face of global recession—and has shifted from being the world's largest food importer to a net exporter as it improved agricultural incentives. China, whose population of one billion and rigid ideology seemed destined to block its economic prospects, has begun to record high growth rates as it decentralized decision making and increased its reliance on the price mechanism (especially in agriculture).

Fourth, the starting point in Latin America is much better than is frequently realized. Savings rates, despite recent declines, are quite high. Governments are effective providers of social services in Latin America which, despite wide country variations, are comparable to those in other developing countries at similar income levels. The same thing cannot be said about their effectiveness as producers and regulators (chapter 4). Economic infrastructure has been established in the advanced countries of the region. Export expansion has been impressive in several cases: Brazil now sells aircraft to the United States, and Argentina sells turbines for electricity plants in the international market. The successes of the 1960s and 1970s inevitably left positive results, along with the buildup of imbalances and inefficiencies that brought them to a halt.

Fifth, policy change in the needed directions is already beginning to occur. Under the pressure of the crisis, virtually every country in Latin America has at least begun to reevaluate its development strategy and policy. Several countries have adopted competitive exchange rates. Some have begun to consider reducing trade protection. Mexico has joined the General Agreement on Tariffs and Trade (GATT).

Some countries have begun to privatize state-owned industry. Argentina and Brazil have launched sweeping monetary reforms. Several countries are reviewing their laws which deter foreign investment, and some of them have signed the convention establishing the World Bank's Multilateral Investment Guarantee Agency (MIGA).

Finally, improvements have occurred in the global environment which are supportive of reform in Latin America. World inflation is down sharply and seems likely to remain there; this promises greater stability and obviates the need for industrial countries to adopt restrictive economic policies. World interest rates have declined, cutting the cost of debt service and promoting more rapid growth. The fall in the price of oil, while hurting Mexico, Venezuela, and Ecuador, brings substantial direct benefit to the rest of the region and indirect benefit to all its countries by further checking inflation and enhancing prospects for faster growth in the world economy. The large decline in the exchange rate of the dollar brings major benefits to the region.

Moreover, the GATT membership seems headed toward a new round of multilateral trade negotiations which could help reverse the protectionist trend and expand market access for Latin American exports. The "Baker Plan" represents a start toward renewing capital flows to the region. To be sure, there are substantial uncertainties in the global outlook and further measures need to be taken by the United States and other industrial countries to obtain a positive outcome, as suggested in our final section. Nevertheless, the international framework is sufficiently hospitable to add to the prospects of success for a new development strategy for Latin America.

Toward Renewed Growth

A new strategy is thus both urgently needed and demonstrably feasible. Such strategies have worked elsewhere. They have even worked in Latin America. The world environment is reasonably favorable. The overriding issue is to find the proper strategy, and to implement it effectively and on a sustained basis.

Latin America has experimented with several development strategies in the past. The most pervasive was the "import-substitution model," emerging from the experiences of the Great Depression and World War II and espoused by the United Nations Economic Commission for Latin America (ECLA) in the 1950s. This approach worked for a while, partly due to favorable global conditions. But reliance on this model soon confronted market limitations (chapter 1); also, Latin America was slow to adjust to the evolving postwar environment, and new approaches were required.

Several strategies were tried in the 1960s. Elements of outward orientation, to be emphasized below, have appeared in several countries for some periods of time. Statist models from both the political left and right, as well as from the military, represented another set of experiments. Monetarist approaches were tried in Argentina, Chile, and Uruguay in the late 1970s. Economic integration of the continent captivated the imagination of many (but was never effectively implemented).

Our recommendations will draw on previous worthwhile efforts; in this sense, our proposals will not always be "new." But none of them were applied within a coherent, comprehensive framework. Even more important, none were maintained for the extended period essential for self-sustaining development to take hold and prosper. Our goal is to propose an overall strategy that will work economically, prove sustainable politically, improve income distribution and social conditions, and perhaps even capture the imagination of a hemisphere where both need and opportunity are now so great.

One key element in this basic strategy must be underlined: the need for *continuity* of policy. No country can succeed economically if it alters its basic strategy every few years, especially if those alterations are in substantially different directions as in many Latin

American countries over the past several decades. Entrepreneurs can plan with confidence, and invest for the long term, only if they can foresee a reasonably stable policy environment.

The alternative, all too frequent throughout the developing world including Latin America, is radical shifts in policy which destroy any plausible basis for sustained development. Adjustments will, of course, be required as external conditions change and the country itself evolves. But consistency and continuity, of both purpose and overall policy direction, are central to our proposed approach.

A Three-Part Strategy

Our proposed strategy contains three central elements for the Latin American countries themselves: outward orientation of the economy, with emphasis on exports and efficient import substitution; the generation of adequate levels of savings, primarily from domestic sources but from abroad as well, and their efficient investment; and a reorientation of the role of government toward its demonstrated comparative advantage of providing services and a framework for economic activity, limiting its role as regulator and producer. The critical fourth element is supportive policy by the industrial countries, notably the United States. The four parts interrelate closely, and all are essential to launch a successful development strategy for Latin America.

Outward orientation is a system of incentives that stimulates exports and efficient import substitution. Only such a focus will enable the countries of the region to achieve self-sustaining growth and simultaneously to service their external debt, because only such a strategy will generate both the needed foreign exchange and the essential stimulus to domestic production.

Outward orientation is the keystone of the strategies of virtually all the "success stories" cited above—in East and Southeast Asia, in Latin America in certain periods, in Turkey, and elsewhere. Even where success has been limited, as in Africa, relatively outward-oriented countries have done much better than the inward-oriented.

Outward orientation is particularly critical for small countries of

Latin America that have limited internal markets. But the experience of medium-sized countries, such as Argentina and Mexico, also points to the conclusion that sustained outward orientation is a sine qua non for successful development—even without the constraint of a heavy external debt, and certainly in the face of such a constraint. Even Brazil, by far the largest country in Latin America, turned increasingly outward in the mid-1960s and continues to provide extensive incentives to export activity.

Questions are sometimes raised as to whether the industrial countries will be willing to accept enough additional imports from Latin America to make outward orientation a feasible, however desirable, strategy for the continent as a whole (table 5.2). Our answer to this question is firmly positive.

To be sure, there has been a disturbing trend toward increased protection in the United States and some other industrial countries. But the volume of manufactured exports of the developing countries, including those from Latin America, increased at a compound annual rate of 11 percent between 1973 and 1983—despite the "rise in protection." At the end of this period, developing countries still supplied only 2.3 percent of consumption of manufactured goods in the industrial world (3.0 percent in the United States). The share of Latin American manufactured exports in total consumption in the industrial countries was only 0.2 percent (though it is of course higher in some specific sectors). Even if these exports continued to grow by 11 percent a year in real terms until the end of the century, and the industrial countries' consumption rose by 3 percent annually, Latin American exports would still meet only 0.8 percent of final demand for manufactured goods in the member countries of the Organization for Economic Cooperation and Development (OECD).

Moreover, Latin American countries can increase their exports to each other and to other areas of the world outside the OECD. If the forthcoming multilateral trade negotiations further reduce import barriers, and especially if they place effective constraints on the use of safeguard measures, their export prospects will be even brighter. There is much room for expanded exports of manufactured products from Latin America, and the demand side of the equation will not be a major constraint.

Most of the Latin American countries will continue to rely at least partially on export of primary products, however. Hence, the outlook for commodity prices is also important in assessing the feasibility of export-led growth.

One cannot predict with confidence any early upturn of significance in these prices, although such a development is by no means impossible. It is quite unlikely, however, that future declines will be sizeable if they occur at all. Moreover, the volume of nonfuel primary exports by developing countries has continued to grow in the early 1980s and this trend is expected to persist. In addition, there is considerable scope for diversification within the primary sector. And development itself implies a steady shift away from primary products toward manufactures (as the industrial countries continue to shift from manufacturing to services). The global outlook for commodities should not be a deterrent to adoption of strategies of outward orientation.

Outward orientation requires several specific types of policies. Some of these apply directly to external economic transactions. Others apply to their domestic underpinnings. Both are essential, and both must be carried out on a sustained basis if outward orientation is to succeed.

The first requirement is *the establishment and maintenance of a competitive exchange rate.* An overvalued currency discourages exports and efficient import substitution. Entrepreneurs will not make the investments needed to achieve international competitiveness if they doubt the authorities' commitment to maintain a competitive exchange rate.

It is not enough to bring the currency into line periodically and then let it slip back into overvaluation, as Mexico did after 1982. Maintaining a competitive exchange rate is critical to convey the proper market signals for investment and production decisions. One way to do this is to adopt crawling-peg regimes, in which the domestic currency is linked to a basket of foreign currencies (reflecting its trading patterns, not the dollar alone), with the exchange rate adjusted continuously to offset inflation differentials and any substantial alterations (such as oil shocks) in the underlying competitive position.

Closely related to proper exchange rate policy is the choice of *appropriate trade policies.* Excessive import protection can undermine efforts to achieve successful export orientation, both because needed inputs are unavailable and because incorrect price signals are perpetuated.

Effective exchange rate policies and effective trade policies reinforce each other. Devaluation provides an opportunity to reduce import barriers without undue adjustment cost in domestic industries, and efficient import-substituting activities are encouraged by a competitive exchange rate. Indeed, beyond promoting exports, a devaluation provides incentives for efficient import-substituting activities that have previously received little or no protection, in both agriculture and manufacturing.

Import substitution can thus be an integral part of an outward-oriented trade policy as long as it meets efficiency criteria. Traditional infant-industry considerations also continue to apply: temporary and degressive protection is legitimate, indeed desirable, where it will foster productive enterprises that will be able to compete without such help within a reasonable period of time. Such protection is better extended through tariffs, not quantitative restrictions, to maximize reliance on price signals and avoid excessive costs.

There are also infant activities in agriculture that may need governmental assistance—such as research into new production techniques and extension services. Eliminating controls on agricultural producer prices will also give a boost to output. Furthermore, import competition through trade liberalization will permit the elimination of price controls on manufactured goods which, while intended to subsidize urban consumption or limit excess profits generated by protection, in fact limit production itself.

Internationally acceptable export incentives are also an essential component of a strategy of outward orientation. Export credit must be available on competitive terms. Imported inputs for export production should be freed from all duties and indirect taxes. Export promotion measures, including information services and trade fairs, can be useful. These proposals for outward-oriented exchange rate and trade policies are developed in chapter 2.

Policies of outward orientation aimed at promoting exports and efficient import substitution, while essential, make up only part of the proposed strategy. The rationalization and modernization of the domestic economy further require *generating higher levels of savings*, primarily domestic but also from abroad, and especially *using all savings available much more efficiently* than in the past.

Yet savings from both domestic and external sources have dropped sharply in most Latin American countries in the 1980s, and new policies to reverse that trend are essential. In addition, comparative capital-output ratios suggest that Latin America uses its resources much less effectively than do rapidly growing developing countries.

Export expansion will generally promote savings, as a higher than average share of export earnings is normally saved. A resumption of growth will itself generate increased savings and could launch a virtuous cycle between the two. But a key part of the proposed strategy is the adoption of new measures to promote higher levels of savings and more efficient investment patterns.

For some time to come, the inflow of new capital may not fully offset interest payments on the external debt, and therefore the net outward transfer of resources will continue. Excess capacity will initially provide the basis for increased exports and domestic growth, but new investment will be needed to expand capacity over time. A resumption of growth thus will require a sustained increase in domestic savings to achieve a sustained increase in domestic investment.

At the same time, policy should aim to induce reversal of capital flight and renewed inflows of foreign capital—particularly in equity and other nondebt-creating forms, to limit any new buildup of external liabilities. As with trade, this will require a series of measures aimed directly at such investment: liberalization of rules governing foreign direct investment and participation in local equity markets, creation of mutual funds (like the Korea Fund and Mexico Fund) to facilitate such investment, perhaps the creation of new "repatriation funds." Latin American countries should join MIGA and accept a wider role for international arbitration in resolving disputes concerning foreign direct investment; such a reversal of traditional attitudes would greatly encourage renewed capital inflows from abroad. However, it must be recognized that sustained and continued capital inflow, be it foreign or flight capital, will occur only over time as a result of consistent application of policies, such as those recommended here, that provide a stable and profitable environment for productive investment.

Foreign direct investment could be a particularly valuable component of an outward-oriented strategy because of the international marketing skills of the multinational companies and their ability to help fight protectionist pressures in their home countries. It is ironic that most countries of Latin America strongly preferred bank loans to foreign equity investment in the 1970s, in pursuit of greater independence from foreign influence, yet would have suffered much less disruption had they chosen the opposite course. Increased reliance on equity flows is both desirable and essential because alternative sources of private funds are unlikely to be available in the future.

The key to both expanding domestic savings and renewing capital inflows from abroad, as noted, lies in changing financial policies in the Latin American countries. Real interest rates, like real exchange rates, have frequently been permitted to sink below levels needed to generate savings (and keep domestic capital at home)—and have even turned negative for protracted periods. Crises have then prompted swings to interest-rate levels which are much too high to foster adequate investment.

A central element in the proposed approach is to assure that *real interest rates remain sufficiently positive* to induce a stable and substantial level of domestic savings and keep most of those savings at home, but not so high as to discourage productive investment. Such market-oriented interest rates are also central to an efficient allocation of investment and thus to the fundamental goal of achieving international competitiveness.

Improvement in national capital markets and the process of financial intermediation also can help increase the level of savings and the efficiency of their use. At the same time, care must be taken to avoid discrimination against small and medium-sized businesses in the provision of credit. Such firms are major creators of new jobs and are thus critical to any growth strategy.

Tax policy can also boost domestic savings by taxing consumption. While tax incentives to investment should be provided under present conditions, favoritism of capital-intensive activities (as has often occurred in the past) should be avoided to maximize the creation of new jobs.

Another major source of the inadequacy of national savings in many Latin American countries is the dissaving flowing from large and continuing government budget deficits. Private investment, which is essential both for sustained economic growth and improvement of external balances, is often "crowded out" as governments use up too great a share of available resources. Because these budget deficits are often accommodated by monetary policy, they generate rapid rates of inflation which, as noted below, discourage savings and distort investment patterns. *Reducing budget deficits is thus a crucial ingredient of the proposed strategy* (chapter 3).

The third central theme of our proposed strategy is *reforming the role of the state in the economic life of Latin America*. Public dissaving via budget deficits is one aspect of this problem. But the problem runs much deeper, indeed to the core of the economic difficulties of the region.

Due in part to the historical heritage of Latin America, the role of the state has become pervasive in most of its countries (chapter 4). Correspondingly, the private sector has been weakened as the state has assumed increasing importance. Part of the blame lies with the private sector itself: its leaders have all too often turned to the state in times of trouble, thereby adding to the expansion of state power. The time has come to begin reversing this trend, as an essential part of a new growth strategy.

The state in Latin America has come to play three major roles: as regulator, as producer, and as provider of services. The record is, in many respects, positive regarding the third of these functions, and this is where it should focus its efforts in the future.

Even in this area, however, greater attention needs to be given to the provision of basic services for improving the lives of the poor as well as to laying the foundation for long-term growth. One key lesson of the 1980s is that resources are severely limited. Resources spent subsidizing inefficient production by state enterprises are resources that cannot be spent on improving health, education, or basic infrastructure. Resources spent to administer a welter of rules and regulations cannot be spent on teachers or doctors or adequate systems of justice. A reduced role for the state as regulator and producer is necessary not only to improve economic efficiency but also to enable the state to do a better job of providing services for its people.

The state as regulator has stifled much entrepreneurial initiative throughout the region. In several countries, numerous licenses are needed even to begin exporting—hardly an auspicious framework within which to promote outward orientation. In Peru, it recently took 289 days to register a new corporation—compared with four hours in Miami. Labor legislation makes it impossible, or at least extremely costly, to dismiss employees even when staff reductions are essential to stay in business—let alone to become internationally competitive.

Costs of doing business are thus greatly inflated. In particular, these costs block much of the potential for creating small and medium-sized firms—which should be major engines of productivity and creativity. Corruption is fostered. Large sums are wasted by the companies in complying with bureaucratic red tape. And large sums are spent by the governments in administering the same bureaucratic procedures.

This environment of pervasive overregulation, documented in chapter 4, is an important element in creating inefficiency in most Latin American economies. The expanding "informal sector" is perhaps the most obvious result. But lacking access to the facilitative aspects of the law, and to credit and insurance, its opportunity to grow and create jobs is limited. Thus entrepreneurial initiative is discouraged.

This same regulatory environment raises prices internally and discourages the flexibility and adaptability needed to achieve international competitiveness and successful outward orientation. Markets abroad will not wait for licenses to be issued and regulations complied with. Meanwhile, somebody else gets the business.

Substantial deregulation is thus a central feature of our proposed development strategy. The state should set the legal framework, assuring private property rights and avoiding abuses of individual freedom. It should adopt a coherent and effective growth strategy, as proposed here, and macroeconomic and microeconomic policies to carry out that strategy. It should promote more equitable distribution of income through improved provision of basic services and the establishment of a policy environment that facilitates the growth and productivity needed to create more and better paying jobs. And it should do all this to the maximum extent through the adoption of laws and regulations which are applied universally, eschewing case-by-case decision making to the maximum extent possible. Indeed, the trend toward political democratization requires such changes—and is fundamentally incompatible with the traditional heavy hand of state regulation throughout Latin America.

Reforms are also needed to reduce the state's role as a producer, and to begin the inevitably lengthy process of revitalizing the private sector. Public utilities and some state enterprises in basic industries have proved to be efficient in some countries. But the proliferation of state enterprises in the potentially competitive sectors has come to involve substantial inefficiencies. It also conflicts with outward orientation because state firms typically come to rely heavily on the favoritism of the state itself to assure their domestic market shares, discouraging them from competing for markets abroad and instead furthering high import protection to enable them to sell at home.

It is obviously impossible to privatize all state enterprises in the competitive sector overnight, even if that were deemed desirable on economic efficiency grounds. Private capital and management skills are simply not available in sufficient amounts. Some firms, however, can be sold off. A clear movement toward privatization should be set in motion.

The Gains For Latin America

We propose three strategic changes for Latin America—outward orientation, inducements for increased savings and more efficient investment, and a reordering of the role of the state. These changes are interdependent and can be carried out most effectively in parallel. For example, competitive exchange rates and positive real interest rates, along with lower budget deficits and less governmental intrusion into the economy, will raise savings levels and promote their efficient investment. Liberalizing imports will permit abolition of price controls, now needed to avoid excess profits, and investment controls, aimed at avoiding overinvestment in protected sectors.

These changes will support greater international competitiveness, producing growth and jobs as well as export earnings to service foreign debt. Reduced protection and deregulation, together, will also contribute to such results. The stimulus to entrepreneurship attendant upon deregulation, and the increased scope for launching small and medium-sized firms, will create jobs to more than offset the layoffs from cutting back on state enterprises and reducing government regulations.

Furthermore, successful outward orientation will generate economic benefits to offset the losses from phasing out unproductive activities. Existing resources and new domestic investment, augmented by increased foreign investment, would shift to more productive and remunerative sectors. This shift, supported by appropriate tax policies, would usually encompass a move from more capital-intensive to more labor-intensive industries—to exploit the competitive advantage of the region. This process would boost employment and wages. Employment and income will also rise in agriculture, which has suffered discrimination in the past. Also, by reducing the role of the state as regulator and producer, more resources will be freed for use in its preferred role as provider of basic services.

In addition to these three sets of policies for renewing the growth process in Latin America, one central element of shorter run macroeconomic management must be stressed—avoiding rapid rates of inflation. The historical record of development reveals an inverse correlation between inflation and economic growth.

The reasons behind this linkage are clear. Rapid inflation distorts price relationships and produces growing inefficiencies. Savings and, particularly, investment are discouraged. Budget deficits become bloated. Capital flight is promoted.

Indexation seeks to prevent these ill effects of inflation, but at best can achieve partial success in doing so. In addition, indexation has ill effects of its own: it locks in inflation at existing levels, usually converts external shocks (such as higher oil prices) into a corresponding rise in domestic inflation, and saps political will to resist ever higher inflation by appearing to obviate its impact on the population.

Hence a successful attack on inflation is an essential prerequisite to permit effective pursuit of the longer run strategies emphasized in this report (chapter 3). In some cases, traditional austerity measures may be essential and may suffice. In cases of extremely high inflation, full-scale monetary reforms may be required—as recently in Argentina, Bolivia, and Brazil. Whatever methods are used, sustained economic growth will hinge on reasonable internal price stability.

The Role of the Industrial Countries

The growth strategy recommended here for Latin America should be pursued under virtually any foreseeable evolution of the world economy. The need for such reform would in fact be even greater if the world economy soured because Latin America would then find it even more difficult to achieve self-sustaining growth, especially in tandem with continued servicing of the external debt, in the absence of reform.

Nevertheless, the industrial countries can play a crucial role in both encouraging the countries of the region to adopt the proposed strategy and in promoting its success. In today's interdependent world, outward orientation for developing countries can achieve far better results if the industrial countries manage the global economy more effectively. This requires them to pursue six closely related outcomes:

- steady world economic growth, averaging at least 3 percent annually

- avoidance of any new import protection and export subsidization, indeed a renewal of steady liberalization of trade

- avoidance of any renewed surges in real interest rates, and preferably their maintenance at historical levels (2 percent to 3 percent) rather than at the much higher levels of the early 1980s

- avoidance of major misalignments among their own currencies, like the massive dollar overvaluation of the early 1980s

- new infusions of capital to Latin American countries that adopt effective adjustment programs

- more effective leadership, and a stronger resource base, for the international financial institutions, particularly the World Bank.

It is in the direct national interest of the industrial countries themselves to pursue these goals vigorously and successfully.

However, the need to provide a hospitable framework for a reorientation of development strategies in Latin America, and in the Third World generally, should add substantially to the impetus for them to do so.

The developing countries are economically very important to the industrial world. Serious economic disruption in those countries might bring debt defaults and could jeopardize the entire global financial network. Political instability in Latin America, borne of economic instability, could threaten the entire hemisphere. The large stakes of the industrial countries in the Third World should encourage them to step up their effort to manage the global economy more effectively, particularly in areas of direct impact such as trade policy and capital flows.

A successful shift to outward orientation in Latin America would be of great economic benefit to the United States and to all industrial countries. Other developing countries that have succeeded in implementing such a strategy have become large and expanding markets for the exports of industrial countries, and Latin America has great potential in this regard. The strategy for Latin America suggested here is decidedly in the interest of the industrial countries as well.

These considerations apply to all industrial countries, not just the United States. More than one-half of Latin America's trade is with countries other than the United States. Only about one-third of private bank exposure in Latin America comes from the United States. Western Europe, Japan, and Canada have extensive direct interests in the region, as well as overwhelming stakes in global peace and prosperity.

The concerns cited apply particularly to the United States, for four additional reasons. First, the United States must clearly take the lead in forging new cooperative efforts to achieve better functioning of the world economy. To be sure, the United States can do so only by working closely with other industrial countries and by using the functional international organizations—especially the International Monetary Fund (IMF), World Bank, and the GATT. But US leadership is critical in promoting the international framework that would spur the adoption of outward-oriented development strategies in Latin America.

Second, the United States has a major stake in a successful resolution of the contemporary dilemma facing Latin America—

the need to restore self-sustaining growth and simultaneously to maintain servicing of the external debt. In a tangible sense, Latin America represented a market for nearly 20 percent of all US exports of goods and services before the debt crisis erupted—and the sharp drop in those exports contributed importantly to the escalation of the US trade deficit. The extensive exposure of US banks in Latin America represents an ongoing threat to the American financial system. In economic terms alone, both the opportunities offered by Latin America and the threats it poses justify a major effort to create the needed global environment.

Third, the United States has a substantial interest in both the social development and continued democratization of the region. More equitable social conditions, opportunity for advancement, and respect for human rights are of vital importance both in and of themselves and as prerequisites for the establishment of stable democratic regimes. If democracy can become firmly established in Latin America, the prospects for the hemisphere's long-term political stability will be greatly enhanced.

The relationship between economic stability and political stability is, of course, not unidimensional, particularly in the short run. The history of Latin America itself, however, reveals that economic difficulties can create social situations ripe for political instability, and even revolution, from both left and right. Achievement of broad-based, self-sustaining economic growth throughout Latin America could solidify the movement toward democracy. A failure to achieve such progress, let alone continuing stagnation or even a relapse into the morass of default and economic conflict, could have incalculable consequences for social justice and hence the stability of the entire hemisphere.

Fourth, adoption by Latin America of the development strategy proposed here would provide a much stronger foundation for constructive interdependence between the two parts of the hemisphere. The strategy places heavy reliance on market forces, on a mixed economy with a strong broad-based private sector rather than one dominated by the state, and on integration into an international economic framework. It is, at its core, quintessentially pragmatic—seeking to apply the lessons of the past and of other countries to contemporary Latin America.

Although the United States itself does not always abide by these principles, they are at the heart of its own economic experience—

and that of most other economic (and political) success stories, in both the industrial and developing worlds. Their adoption in Latin America would represent an important step that could only improve, over time and to a substantial degree, the relationships— and even the similarity of ways of thinking—between the two parts of the Western Hemisphere.

Proposals for Action

To create a world that offers the best prospects for success of the proposed strategy for Latin America, the United States should both make changes in its own policies and renew its efforts to achieve international agreement to act on several fronts. Fortunately, movement in the needed directions has begun. The critical requirement now is to complete the initiatives undertaken, both for their own sake and to demonstrate to Latin America the enhanced prospects for successful resolution of its own economic dilemma.

Over the next few years, *the United States needs to return to a more balanced mix of fiscal and monetary policy.* Doing so would *produce a further reduction of real interest rates,* which in turn could help *achieve and maintain an equilibrium exchange rate for the dollar.* Such a restoration of dollar equilibrium, with the attendant decline in the US trade deficit, will reduce the pressures for trade protection. The countries of Latin America would benefit greatly from all these effects.

At the same time, the *industrial countries outside the United States—especially Japan and Germany—need to expand domestic demand more rapidly.* This is essential to offset the adverse effect on world growth, and thus trade, of the reductions in the US budget deficit, and to reinforce the adjustment of their currencies against the dollar.

More rapid growth, and currency adjustment, in industrial countries outside the United States is essential for another reason. The United States must improve its trade position by more than $100 billion annually over the next few years, to reduce the risk of protectionist trade policies and the threat of renewed international financial instability, which would result (if the United States sought to maintain annual borrowings of $100 billion or more indefinitely from the rest of the world). Unless other OECD countries, which can afford it, accept the counterpart deterioration in their trade positions, an important portion of that counterpart could fall on Latin America. Its debt problem would then be intensified and its growth prospects adversely affected. A *proper* adjustment of the huge imbalances among OECD countries from the first half of the 1980s is of great importance to Latin America.

In contemplating the adoption of new development strategies, however, the countries of Latin America will look to the longer run and seek to assess whether there are prospects that the proposed approach will work on an enduring basis. This in turn relates to the ongoing effectiveness and stability of the international economic arrangements among the major industrial countries and the attitudes of those countries toward the functioning of such arrangements.

One clear requirement is to avoid further erosion of the international trading system. In light of historical evidence that forward movement toward trade liberalization is needed to avoid backsliding toward protection, it is incumbent on the industrial countries to restart the liberalization process. It is also essential that they begin to enforce GATT rules that seek to avoid or limit trade distortions, and agree on new rules where needed to do so.

The most promising approach is to *launch a new multilateral round of trade negotiations* for the latter 1980s, like the Kennedy Round of the 1960s and the Tokyo Round of the 1970s. Such an initiative would seek to reduce further, and perhaps eliminate over time, the remaining tariffs maintained by industrial countries. It would seek reductions in nontariff barriers, including import quotas, both for sectors that have had controls (such as textiles and steel) and for sectors of newly emerging importance (such as services and intellectual property). It should bring all forms of trade control, including so-called "voluntary export restraint agreements," under international surveillance and limit their use through the institution of a new "safeguards code."

Such reform of the international trading system (chapter 5) could offer substantial assurances to Latin America that its new emphasis on outward orientation would receive support abroad. The regime would retain some preferential treatment for developing countries, including those in Latin America, such as authorization for infant-industry protection under certain circumstances.

Its emphasis, however, would be on bringing those countries into the mainstream of the regime. Their own policy concerns would then receive much greater ongoing weight in managing the system.

For the new trade round to succeed, the more advanced Latin American countries will have to offer reciprocal concessions of their own—though not to the same extent, and not on the same timetable, as the industrial countries. But Latin America would have much to gain from such a negotiation and such a new regime. It could ally with the United States to reduce agricultural protection and to seek limits on the agricultural subsidies offered by the European Community and Japan. It could ally itself with the United States and the European Community to seek the elimination of informal measures of protection in Japan. It could ally with the European Community and Japan to limit the administrative discretion with which the United States applies its "unfair" trade laws. It could ally with other industrializing countries and Japan to check the tendencies of the United States and European Community to apply "voluntary" restraints on their exports. It could use the negotiations and the new regime, including the need to make "concessions" of its own, to provide better access for its exports, to influence the decision-making process in GATT, and to influence its internal debates over trade policy in the direction of import liberalization, which is an important part of the proposed strategy.

The United States already has taken the lead in promoting the inauguration of a new trade round. Most of the other industrial countries seem prepared to cooperate. Ironically, much of the hesitation has come from developing countries—including Brazil and Argentina—which probably have most to gain from the effort. On the other hand, Mexico has decided to reverse its trade policy of forty years and join the GATT. Concerted efforts by the United States and Latin American countries to launch the round, and bring it to a successful conclusion, could add substantially to the proposed strategy for the hemisphere.

A second major area of needed global reform relates to the international monetary system. The regime of unmanaged exchange rate flexibility has permitted substantial currency misalignments to develop. For example, the large dollar overvaluation of the early 1980s severely hurt Latin America's trade competitiveness (because most of its currencies are tied to the dollar), damaged demand for its commodity exports (most of which are priced in dollars), and generated strong pressures for trade protection in the United States. *A reform of the international monetary regime* that could limit the extent of such misalignments would substantially brighten the prospects for outward-oriented development in Latin America.

Such trade and monetary steps by the industrial countries would make a considerable contribution to helping the countries of Latin America deal effectively with their external debt. In addition, however, several measures aimed directly at that problem are in order. For reasons developed in chapter 5, we do not advocate defaults, debt forgiveness, unilateral modification of interest obligations by the debtors (as in Peru at present), or other "radical" approaches—because we believe they would not be in the interest of either debtors in Latin America or creditors elsewhere.

But *new credits will clearly be needed on a scale much larger than now seems forthcoming, probably on the order of $20 billion annually for the next few years.* A large part of these credits will have to come from the commercial banks, and the authorities of industrial countries should encourage such flows—through means including partial guarantees offered by their national export credit agencies and by the multilateral development banks. In addition, where warranted by the performance and policies of the borrowing countries, the banks should negotiate long-term debt restructurings and reduce interest-rate spreads as much as possible.

However, it will take some time for voluntary bank lending to Latin America to resume on any substantial scale. Indeed, all private capital flows to the region are likely to remain modest for some time due both to the continuation of crisis conditions in many countries and to the inevitable time lags in implementing new policies in the region which *inter alia* will attract such flows. Hence, alternative means must be sought.

The obvious source of much of the needed lending in the interim is the international financial institutions, notably the World Bank and Inter-American Development Bank. As financial intermediaries, they can expand their lending without burdening the budgets of creditor governments. They can achieve further multiplier effects through cofinancing and partial guarantees of private loans. Moreover, they can link their loans to policy changes of the type proposed here and thus encourage adoption of the new strategy.

The amounts of new lending envisaged for these institutions by the "Baker Plan," an added $3 billion a year for the 15 major debtors (of which 10 are in Latin America), are much too small. Achieving a substantially larger amount will require a sizeable general capital increase for the World Bank by 1990 or sooner; this can prudently be done without any increase in paid-in capital by the industrial countries, thereby avoiding any impact on their budgets. This approach would be preferable to changing the Bank's gearing ratio, which has also been suggested. Substantial increases in the resources of the Inter-American Development Bank are needed as well.

Fortified with such additional resources, the World Bank should assume a greater role in the lending process—in organizing financial packages based on medium-term adjustment programs and monitoring the implementation of these programs. This would involve an explicit linkage between rescheduling of bank debt, additional financing, and the adoption of a comprehensive reform program. Such a procedure, already used with beneficial effects in the recent cases of Chile and Colombia, can ensure that desirable adjustment measures are taken and that they are supported by additional financing. The IDB, too, will need to move into nonproject lending and link it to policy reforms.

Changes in IMF lending are also needed, in three directions. As has been done in the case of Mexico, the Fund should continue its programs in Latin American countries that maintain effective adjustment efforts. It should establish a new facility to compensate for interest-rate shocks, thus providing credits to offset the adverse effects on debtor countries of any new upswing in interest rates. And it should use the existing compensatory financing facility more extensively, particularly to offset shortfalls in *oil* exports.

For the longer term, new forms of private investment in Latin America should be promoted in the form of equity, quasi-equity, and new types of financial instruments, such as indexed bonds and commodity linked bonds. The Latin American countries can readily stimulate more foreign investment in their stock markets and real estate, for example, by judicious changes in their own policies. (And adoption of the proposed strategy would by itself go far to encourage such investments.) But there will be instances in which industrial countries will need to reduce impediments to such flows from their side of the equation, such as regulatory limitations on the foreign investments of insurance companies and pension funds. The International Finance Corporation can play a particularly useful role in exploring specific possibilities to both the borrowing and the industrial countries, and encouraging the policies needed to exploit them.

There are thus a number of areas in which the United States and other industrial countries can take substantial new initiatives to help foster a welcoming climate for the proposed development strategy in Latin America. All these initiatives are in the interest of the industrial countries themselves. But their adoption could pay substantial dividends in terms of the response from Latin America as well.

Conclusions

Economic reform is imperative in Latin America. A new approach is essential to promote broad-based, self-sustaining growth along with continued servicing of the external debt. A strategy centered on outward orientation, new market incentives for savings and investment, and a fundamental shift in the role of the state can resolve the dilemma.

Adoption of such a strategy will require numerous changes, structural as well as immediate, in both the external and domestic economic policies of the Latin American countries. The prospects for such reform, however, are encouraging. The record of Latin America in the past, and of many other developing countries at present, shows that such policies can succeed. The world environment is improving. Policy changes in the needed direction are beginning to occur within Latin America and in a complementary direction in the industrial countries. The previously entrenched forces of resistance to reform seem to be yielding in the face of crisis.

The stakes for Latin Americans themselves are enormous. The economic future of the continent, and the living conditions of its people for many decades, may be determined by the strategic choices made over the next few years. The prospects for nurturing and extending the move to democracy, and for creating more equitable societies, may rest in the balance.

The stakes for outsiders, particularly the United States, are also extremely high. The national interests of the industrial countries require a stable, prosperous, and democratic Latin America. The proposed strategy could substantially enhance the prospects for achieving these goals on a lasting basis. The industrial countries can contribute greatly to the prospects for adoption and fulfillment of this strategy by modifying their own policies and improving global economic arrangements—all of which are in their own interests in any event.

The two parts of the hemisphere cannot afford not to pursue a strategy along the lines outlined in this report. A failure to resolve the current dilemma constructively could levy huge, lasting costs in both Latin America and the United States. Piecemeal responses to the outbreak of crises, in one country after another, are not adequate. Far-sighted, preemptive, strategic choices must be made soon.

This is our response to skeptics who will observe that several of our proposals have been suggested before, and that some have been tried—however briefly in individual countries. These observers may argue that entrenched advocates of the status quo, or simply inertia, may preclude adoption of our approach.

Such critics, however, would miss the depth and fundamental nature of the crisis of the 1980s. Historic opportunities arise from unprecedented difficulties. Extreme need can overcome deep-seated opposition. We believe that the principles outlined in this report offer a persuasive and feasible strategy for the future and that they can help countries in both parts of our hemisphere to build on the current crisis to forge a new future of success and harmony for all their peoples.

Selected Tables

Table 1.2   Gross domestic product per capita
(dollars)

Country	In 1955 prices			1950
	1929	1937	1950	1950
Argentina	540	510	615	1,877
Brazil	105	145	195	637
Chile	245	280	340	1,416
Colombia	155	175	225	949
Ecuador	n.a.	n.a.	n.a.	638
Mexico	n.a.	230	235	1,055
Peru	n.a.	n.a.	145	953
Uruguay	n.a.	n.a.	n.a.	2,184
Venezuela	n.a.	n.a.	635	2,127
Austria	380	370	450	1,693
Finland	345	430	555	1,972
Italy	275	260	360	1,379
Japan	145	185	135	810
Greece	n.a.	n.a.	(296)	905
Portugal	n.a.	230	285	733
Spain	n.a.	n.a.	(351)	1,163
Turkey	n.a.	n.a.	n.a.	701
Korea	n.a.	n.a.	n.a.	(450)
Singapore	n.a.	n.a.	n.a.	n.a.
Taiwan	n.a.	n.a.	n.a.	508

n.a.   Not available.

Note: Numbers in parenthesis are estimates derived by applying national data on economic growth rates to estimates for later years.

Sources: 1929, 1937, and 1950 (at 1955 prices and exchange rates), Maizels (1963), table E.2; 1950–1980 (1975 prices and purchasing power parities), Summers and Heston (1984), pp. 207–62; 1985 (at 1975 prices and purchasing power parities), 1980 estimates updated by utilizing national data on economic growth rates.

In 1975 prices					1985
1960	1966	1973	1980	1985	1950
2,124	2,359	3,045	3,209	2,719	1.45
912	985	1,624	2,152	2,072	3.25
1,664	1,984	2,108	2,372	2,135	1.51
1,070	1,195	1,536	1,882	1,878	1.99
758	902	1,190	1,556	1,448	2.27
1,401	1,730	2,170	2,547	2,436	2.31
1,200	1,561	1,740	1,746	1,563	1.64
2,501	2,491	2,653	3,269	2,727	1.25
2,839	3,387	3,468	3,310	2,671	1.26
2,764	3,488	4,837	6,052	6,565	3.88
2,912	3,659	5,129	5,939	6,593	3.34
2,313	2,962	3,971	4,661	4,808	3.49
1,674	2,810	5,025	5,996	7,130	8.80
1,385	2,024	3,334	3,946	3,990	4.41
1,137	1,501	2,615	3,092	3,155	4.30
1,737	2,730	3,841	4,264	4,336	3.73
1,044	1,262	1,586	2,069	2,347	3.35
631	798	1,356	2,007	2,648	5.88
1,054	1,306	2,689	3,948	5,001	n.a.
733	1,005	1,691	2,522	3,160	6.22

Table 1.3   **Manufactured exports per capita**
            (dollars)

Country	1960	1966	1973	1983	1984
Argentina	2	4	29	43	47
Brazil	0	1	12	68	n.a.
Chile	n.a.	5	5	30	n.a.
Colombia	0	2	14	20	19
Ecuador	n.a.	1	2	8	n.a.
Mexico	3	4	20	33	n.a.
Peru	0	0	2	n.a.	n.a.
Uruguay	n.a.	5	18	99	n.a.
Venezuela	n.a.	1	5	n.a.	n.a.
Austria	n.a.	176	571	1,730	1,765
Finland	106	195	568	1,919	2,029
Italy	54	121	336	1,085	1,094
Japan	34	89	320	1,179	1,362
Greece	2	7	60	219	237
Portugal	19	42	143	333	386
Spain	4	17	92	359	416
Turkey	0	0	6	56	80
Korea	0	5	79	556	657
Singapore	14	44	456	2,415	2,911
Taiwan	5	21	238	1,199	n.a.

n.a.   Not available.

Note: Manufacturing exports have been defined as Classes 5 to 8 less 68 in the Standard International Trade Classification, thus excluding processed foods, beverages, and tobacco as well as nonferrous metals.

Source: GATT trade tapes.

Table 1.5 Debt servicing and inflation

Country	Interest payments as percentage of exports, 1985	Debt-export ratio, 1985	Inflation rate	
			1981	Mid–1985
Argentina	55	5.9	105	1,130
Brazil	44	4.0	106	217
Chile	47	5.3	20	35
Colombia	23	2.7	27	28
Ecuador	25	2.6	13	30
Mexico	37	4.5	28	53
Peru	35	4.5	75	169
Uruguay	36	5.6	34	70
Venezuela	23	2.1	16	13

Source: For interest payments and debt-export ratios, ECLA (1985b); for inflation rates, IMF, *International Financial Statistics,* various issues.

Table 2.1 **Real effective exchange rates**
(1976–78 = 100)

Country	1971	1972	1973	1974	1975	1976	1977
Argentina	92.1	105.2	98.6	87.2	118.9	90.3	110.2
Brazil	92.0	95.6	103.9	103.0	103.3	98.6	97.9
Chile	67.3	51.1	44.3	86.7	113.2	99.4	92.7
Colombia	112.6	114.1	115.8	109.7	112.6	106.8	96.1
Ecuador	126.4	128.0	136.2	123.4	114.7	103.3	101.8
Mexico	91.9	94.9	95.4	92.1	90.4	93.9	105.2
Peru	74.5	75.7	83.0	82.5	74.6	79.8	94.4
Uruguay	86.4	106.2	94.8	84.4	96.6	101.1	99.9
Venezuela	98.2	99.5	106.7	109.3	104.6	101.2	98.1

n.a.   Not available.

Note: Trade-weighted exchange rates, adjusted for changes in wholesale prices at home and abroad, except for Chile where the adjusted consumer price index was used until 1975, because of the lack of reliability of wholesale price indices for the period. (An increase in the index represents a depreciation, a decline an appreciation, of real effective exchange rates.)

Source: IMF, *International Financial Statistics*, various issues.

1978	1979	1980	1981	1982	1983	1984	1985
99.4	75.7	67.5	75.6	115.2	103.6	95.7	129.4
103.5	114.9	127.6	103.8	98.3	115.7	109.2	109.6
107.8	98.5	83.8	75.3	83.9	90.5	91.4	103.8
97.1	94.7	95.9	88.9	81.1	79.8	85.3	95.8
95.0	97.5	105.1	102.3	103.0	130.5	152.1	131.2
100.9	96.7	89.0	80.1	115.0	121.0	100.3	98.0
125.9	124.1	114.0	96.5	92.4	100.3	101.1	121.0
99.0	84.7	77.6	73.7	76.9	105.3	96.5	95.4
100.7	104.2	98.6	89.5	81.8	76.6	106.7	96.3

Table 3.1   **Savings or investment ratios**
(percentage of GDP)

Country	Savings on investment	1960–66	1967–73	1974–80	1981–84
Argentina	GDS	19.4	21.2	26.4	19.0
	FS	0.2	−1.0	−1.5	−3.0
	GDI	19.6	20.2	24.9	16.0
Brazil	GDS	24.8	24.8	23.9	20.5
	FS	−0.4	0.8	2.6	−1.7
	GDI	24.4	25.6	26.5	18.8
Chile	GDS	13.2	13.9	15.6	10.0
	FS	1.3	0.2	1.3	3.0
	GDI	14.5	14.1	16.9	13.0
Colombia	GDS	16.7	17.8	20.2	16.1
	FS	1.0	1.0	−1.6	3.8
	GDI	17.6	18.8	18.6	19.9
Ecuador	GDS	11.1	14.8	24.1	22.7
	FS	2.6	4.3	1.6	−1.3
	GDI	13.6	19.1	25.6	21.4
Mexico	GDS	18.7	20.2	23.0	28.4
	FS	1.1	1.2	1.3	−5.6
	GDI	19.8	21.2	24.2	22.8
Peru	GDS	23.2	16.4	15.9	15.6
	FS	−0.2	−0.8	0.9	0.3
	GDI	22.9	15.5	16.8	15.9
Uruguay	GDS	14.5	12.5	11.9	12.2
	FS	−0.6	−0.6	3.2	0.2
	GDI	13.9	11.9	15.1	12.4
Venezuela	GDS	35.4	34.7	36.2	25.8
	FS	−13.9	−6.6	−3.3	−6.6
	GDI	21.5	28.2	32.8	19.1

Country	Savings on investment	1960–66	1967–73	1974–80	1981–84
Austria	GDS	28.0	29.4	26.9	24.0
	FS	−0.3	−0.4	0.9	−0.5
	GDI	27.7	29.0	27.8	23.5
Finland	GDS	24.8	26.5	26.6	25.7
	FS	1.2	0.3	0.9	−1.6
	GDI	26.7	26.8	27.5	24.6
Italy	GDS	23.6	22.4	22.1	18.3
	FS	−0.3	−0.8	0.5	0.7
	GDI	23.3	21.6	22.6	19.0
Japan	GDS	34.7	38.2	33.1	31.4
	FS	−0.2	−1.3	−0.2	−1.7
	GDI	34.5	36.9	32.9	29.7
Greece	GDS	14.1	19.0	18.9	15.7
	FS	8.3	8.7	8.1	8.6
	GDI	22.2	27.5	27.9	22.3
Portugal	GDS	18.5	20.2	14.6	16.4
	FS	5.8	5.2	13.5	14.9
	GDI	24.7	26.4	28.8	31.3
Spain	GDS	21.6	23.0	21.0	19.3
	FS	1.1	1.1	2.4	0.3
	GDI	22.6	24.0	23.4	19.6
Turkey	GDS	13.1	16.2	15.4	15.2
	FS	2.6	2.5	6.6	5.7
	GDI	15.7	18.6	22.1	20.9
Korea	GDS	5.4	16.0	24.3	25.8
	FS	9.5	9.0	6.1	2.0
	GDI	15.2	25.1	30.4	27.8

(continued overleaf)

Table 3.1   *Continued*
(percentage of GDP)

Country	Savings on investment	1960–66	1967–73	1974–80	1981–84
Singapore	GDS	8.6	20.4	31.7	40.8
	FS	8.7	13.5	8.5	4.6
	GDI	16.7	33.6	40.5	45.5
Taiwan	GDS	16.6	27.1	32.6	32.1
	FS	3.3	−1.2	−0.3	−7.2
	GDI	19.9	25.9	32.2	25.0

GDS   gross domestic savings. FS   foreign savings, defined to equal net capital flows, interest payments, and dividends. GDI   gross domestic investment. Interest payments and dividends are considered to be part of the gross domestic product, not the gross national product.

Source: IMF, *International Financial Statistics,* various issues.

Table 4.1   Growth of the public sector, 1970–82

Country	Public-sector outlays as percentage of GDP		Of which state enterprises		Estimated share of state enterprises in gross domestic investment	Public-sector deficit as percentage of GDP	
	1970	1982[a]	1970	1982	(1978–80)	1970	1982
Argentina	33	35	11	12	20	1	14
Brazil	28	32	6	11	39	2	17
Chile	41	36	5	10	13	5	2
Colombia	26	30	6	10	9	4	2
Mexico	21	48	10	26	24	2	17
Peru	25	57	4	32	15	1	9
Venezuela	32	66	17	45	45	3	4
Weighted average	28	42	9	19	29	2	9
Malaysia	36	53	4	34	33	12	19
Korea	20	28	7	4	23	4	3
France	38	48	6	7	13	0.5	3
Japan	23	27	8	8	11	1.5	6
Sweden	52	66	4	6	11	2	10
United Kingdom	43	49	10	11	17	3	6
United States	22	21	10	9	4	1	2

Note: The peak figures for Argentina were 42 percent and for Brazil 35 percent; both pertain to 1981.

Source: IDB (1984), Appendix on Public Finances; IMF (1985); Short (1984); Cline (1985–86): national statistics for Asian and European countries.

Table 4.3   **State economic regulations**

Regulation (1985)	Argentina	Brazil
Price controls, nine basic staples[a] (number)	9.0	9
Price controls, five basic manufactures[b] (number)	5.0	5
Mandatory ceilings on bank interest rates (yes or no)	yes	yes
Foreign direct investment limitation in		
Industrial companies (yes or no)	no	no
Banks (yes or no)	yes	yes
Maximum domestic corporate profits tax rate (percentage)	33.0	35
Withholding on after-tax profits remitted abroad[d] (percentage)	17.5	25
Workers' mandatory profitsharing in industrial companies (yes or no)	yes	yes
Fringe benefits as percentage of average industrial wage	80	80
Limitations on reductions on employment (significant or insignificant)	S	I

Source: "Investing, Licensing, Trading Conditions Abroad," Business International Corporation data for Argentina February 1985, for Brazil January 1985, for Chile October 1985, and for Peru March 1985; "Doing Business in Chile," Price Waterhouse, October 1985; "Doing Business in Mexico," Price Waterhouse, June 1984; "Doing Business in Venezuela," Price Waterhouse, August 1985.

a.   Wheat, bread, meat, poultry, sugar, vegetable oil, milk, soft drinks, basic pharmaceuticals.

b.   Cement, steel, cars and trucks, fertilizer, and tires.

c.   First-category tax of 10 percent levied on income, 30 percent levied on taxable income net of first-catego.

d.   In addition to profits tax.

Chile	Colombia	Mexico	Peru	Venezuela
0	9	5	9	9
0	5	5	5	3
yes	yes	yes	yes	no
no	yes	yes	yes	yes
no	yes	yes	yes	yes
30ᶜ	40	42	50	50
40	40	55	40	20
no	no	yes	yes	yes
65	65	60	50	60
I	S	S	S	S

Table 4.5 **Social welfare indicators**

	Argentina		Brazil		Chile		Colombia	
	1960	1980	1960	1980	1960	1980	1960	1980
Average life expectancy at birth (years)	65	70	55	63	57	67	53	63
Infant mortality (per 1,000 live births)	61	45	118	77	114	43	93	56
Population (per doctor)	740	530	2,210	1,700	1,780	1,930	2,640	1,710
Population (per medical assistant)	750	n.a.	2,810	820	640	450	4,220	800
Percentage of minimum daily calorie requirements supplied	n.a.	125	n.a.	109	n.a.	114	n.a.	108
Enrollment in school (percentage of age group)								
Primary	98	116	95	93	109	117	77	128
Secondary	23	56	11	32	24	55	12	46
Adult literacy rate (percentage)	91	93	61	76	84	n.a.	63	81
Energy consumption per capita (kg coal equivalent per year)	1,177	2,161	385	1,102	833	1,137	519	970
Electricity consumption per capita (kw/hour)	513	1,406	325	1,149	598	1,058	244	890
Percentage of population with access to piped water	51	58	32	56	63	78	54	56

n.a   Not available.

Source: Government compilations by the IDB; special communications.

Ecuador		Mexico		Peru		Uruguay		Venezuela		Upper middle-income countries	
1960	1980	1960	1980	1960	1980	1960	1980	1960	1980	1960	1980
51	61	58	65	47	58	68	71	57	67	57	60
140	82	91	56	163	88	50	40	85	42	103	62
2,670	760	1,830	1,260	1,910	1,390	960	540	1,510	990	2,606	1,689
2,360	570	3,650	1,420	3,530	970	800	190	2,840	380	2,678	1,010
n.a.	88	n.a.	121	n.a.	99	n.a.	110	n.a.	112	n.a.	115
83	107	80	120	83	112	111	105	100	104	88	104
12	40	11	37	15	56	37	60	21	39	20	48
68	81	65	83	61	80	n.a.	94	63	82	61	76
216	692	786	1,684	433	807	1,020	1,160	3,014	3,039	798	1,677
n.a.	n.a.	313	972	265	567	n.a.	n.a.	601	2,298	n.a.	n.a.
n.a.	57	38	50	45	51	n.a.	80.4	50	80	n.a.	n.a.

Table 5.2   **Relative importance of manufactured imports from developing countries**
(ratio of imports to the consumption of manufacture of goods, current prices)

Importer	1973	1978	1981	1983
United States				
Iron and steel	0.6	0.9	1.4	2.3
Chemicals	0.4	0.5	0.6	0.9
Other semimanufactures	0.9	1.5	1.7	1.9
Engineering products	0.7	1.3	2.0	2.6
Textiles	1.8	1.6	2.3	2.2
Clothing	5.6	11.3	14.0	15.1
Other consumer goods	1.9	3.7	4.8	5.2
All manufactures	1.1	1.8	2.4	3.0
European Community				
Iron and steel	0.4	0.4	0.6	0.7
Chemicals	0.5	0.6	0.8	1.1
Other semimanufactures	1.3	2.5	1.9	2.3
Engineering products	0.3	0.9	1.3	1.4
Textiles	2.6	3.7	4.1	4.4
Clothing	5.7	11.4	16.4	16.0
Other consumer goods	1.1	1.6	2.9	3.1
All manufactures	0.9	1.6	2.0	2.1
Japan				
Iron and steel	0.2	0.3	1.0	1.6
Chemicals	0.3	0.5	0.8	0.9
Other semimanufactures	1.0	0.9	0.9	0.9
Engineering products	0.2	0.3	0.5	0.4
Textiles	2.2	2.3	2.1	1.9
Clothing	7.6	7.4	8.9	8.2
Other consumer goods	0.8	1.1	1.3	1.5
All manufactures	0.7	0.8	0.9	1.0

Source: GATT, *International Trade;* United Nations, *Yearbook of Industrial Statistics;* and OECD, *Indicators of Industrial Activity,* various years.

Appendix A   Individuals consulted in Latin America concerning this study

Business

ARGENTINA

Jorge Aceiro
President
Río Colorado (Bridas)

Guillermo Alchourron
President
Sociedad Rural Argentina

Carlos Pedro Blaquier
President
Ledesma, S.A.

José Roberto Canton
President
Stock Exchange

Carlos Carballo
President
Banco Finamerica, S.A.

Luis Cetra
Director
Diario Tiempo Argentino

Carlos Dietl
President
Petroquímica Argentina, S.A.
  (PASA)

Roberto Favelevic
President
Industrial Union

Luis Maria Flynn
President
Cargill, S.A.

Ernesto Grether
President
Cámara Argentina de Comercio

Ricardo Gruneisen
President
ASTRA, S.A.

Roque Maccarone
President
Asociación de Bancos Argentinos

Rodolfo Martelli
President
Bank Roberts, S.A.

Luis M. Otero Monsegur
President
Banco Francés del Río de la Plata

Enrique Nosiglia
Adviser
Consejo Asesor para la
  Consolidación de la Democracia

Roberto Rocca
President
TECHINT, S.A.

Carlos Videla
President, Argentine Chapter
Consejo Interamericano del
  Comercio y Producción
  (CICYP)

Federico Zorraquin
President
Banco Comercial del Norte

The views expressed in this report are not necessarily those of the individuals consulted or of the organizations they represent.

BRAZIL
André de Botton
President
Mesbla, S.A.

Keith Bush
Director
São Paulo Alpargatas, S.A.

Rodrigo de Pádua Lopes
President
Dragagem Fluvial, S.A.

Jacky Delmar
President
Brascan Imobiliaria, S.A.

Arthur Joáo Donata
President
Federacão das Indústrias do Rio de
    Janeiro

Geraldo de Figueiredo Forbes
President
Finacorp Ltda.

Peter Landsberg
President
Verolme—Estaleiros Reuindos do
    Brazil, S.A

Roberto Maluf
President and Chief Executive
    Officer
Eucatex, S.A.—Industria e
    Comercio

Marcilio Marques Moreira
Vice President
União de Bancos Brasileros, S.A.
    (Unibanco)

José Mindlin
President
Metal Leve, S.A.

Sergio Quintella
President
Internacional de Engenharia, S.A.

Roberto Teixeira da Costa
President
Brasilpar Comércio e
    Participaçóes, S.A.

Amaury Temporal
President
Asociacão Comercial do Rio de
    Janeiro

CHILE
Anacleto Angelini
Agent
Industrias Pesqueras y otras

Elías Brugere
President
Cámara de Comercio Minorista

Alvaro Donoso
Economist, Former Director
Bureau for National Planning

Jorge Fontaine
President
Confederación de la Producción y
    del Comercio

Jaime Guzmán
Chief Legal Counsel
Partido U.D.I.

Felipe Lamarca
Economist
Businessman

Elidoro Matte
President
Banco Industrial y Comercio
    Exterior (BICE)

Hermógenes Perez de Arce
Lawyer and Journalist

Manuel Valdés
President
Sociedad Nacional de Agricultura

COLOMBIA
Jaime Lizarralde Lora
Former President
Celanese Corporation

COSTA RICA
Edmondo Gerli G.
President
Botica Francesa

MEXICO
Jorge Chapa Salazar
Former President
Management Advisory Council

Mario Garza González
Director of Public Relations
Grupo VITRO, S.A.

Alejandro Garza Laguera
President of the Advisory Council
Cigarrera la Moderna, S.A.

Bernardo Garza Sada
President and Executive Director of
  the Council
General Grupo ALFA, S.A

Andrés Marcelo Sada Zambrano
General Director
Celulosa y Derivados, S.A.
  (CYDSA)

Francisco Patiño Leal
General Director
Banco Mercantil del Norte

Alberto Santos de Hoyos
President, Grupo Gallertera
  Méxicana (GAMESA) and
Member, Comité Asesor Industrial
  de la Presidencia de la República

Guillermo Velasco Arzac
Secretary of the Director's Council
Confederación Patonal de la
  República Méxicana
  (COPARMEX)

Lorenzo Zambrano Trevíno
General Director
Cementos Mexicanos

NICARAGUA
Ramiro Gurdian
President
Nicaraguan Agricultural Federation

PANAMA
Rafael Arosemena
Vice President
Asociación Bancaria Panameña

José Chirino
President
Pepsi Cola

Carol V. de Montenegro
President
Feria Internacional de Agricultura,
  Ganadería, Pesca, y Alimentación

Alberto C. Motta
Manager
Motta International, S.A.

George Richa
Former President
Sindicato de Industriales de Panamá

J.J. Vallarino Jr.
President
Coca Cola, Panama
Continental President
Consejo Interamericano del
  Comercio y Producción (CICYP)

PERU
Antonio Aguirre Roca
President of the Board of Directors
Fábrica de Eternit, S.A.

Ernesto Baertl Montori
General Managing Director
Cía Minera Milpa, S.A.

Luis Paz Silva
President
Fundación Nacional de Desarrollo

Walter Piazza
Executive President
COSAPI, S.A.
Ingenieros Contratistas

Julio Piccini
President
Compañía Constructora Upaca, S.A.

Ramón Remolina
Consultant
Banco de Crédito

URUGUAY
Ernesto Julio Carrau
President
Carrau Hermanos

VENEZUELA
Rafael Alfonso
President
Caracas Industrial Council

Roger Boulton
Director
Boulton Group

Vincente Brito
President
Managas Industrial Council

Antonio Herrera Vaillant
Director for Institutional Relations
Organización Diego Cisneros

Freddy Muller Borges
Lawyer, and Former President
Tamanaco Hotel

Noel Teale James
President
Publicidad Corpa

Mario Palenzona
President
Palenzono Laboratories

John P. Phelps
Director
Sindicato Phelps

Carlos Guillermo Rangel
Executive Vice President
La Metropolitana

Arnando Sehwerert
Executive Director
Venezuelan Pharmaceutical
    Association

Economics

ARGENTINA
Alvaro Alsogaray
Congressman

Guido Di Tella
Economist
University Professor

Luis María Dagnino Pastore
Former Minister of Economics

Adalbert Krieger Vasena
Former Minister of Economics

Marcos Victoria
President
Instituto de Estudios
    Contemporáneos

Javier Villanueva
Professor
Catholic University

BRAZIL
Antonio Carlos Porto Gonçalves
Economist
Fundação Getúlio Vargas

CHILE
Eduardo Aninat
Economics Consultant

Pablo Baraona
Economist
Former Minister of Economics

Jorge Desormeaux
Professor of Economics
Catholic University

Carlos Hurtado
Economic Consultant

Carlos Massad
Former President, UNECLA
Central Bank of Chile

MEXICO
Everado Elizondo
Director of Economic Studies
Cámara de la Industria de
  Transformación (CAINTRA)

Rolando Espinoza
Director
Centro de Estudios en
  Economía y Educación

Rafael Garza Berlanga
Professor
University of Monterrey

Edgardo Reyers Salcido
Director of Special Studies
Grupo Vallores Industriales, S.A.
  (VISA)

PERU
Ivan Alonso
Manager, Business Department
Instituto Libertad y Democracia

Hernando de Soto
President
Instituto Libertad y Democracia

Luis Morales Bayro
Manager, Economics Department
Instituto Libertad y Democracia

María Murillo
Manager, Housing Department
Instituto Libertad y Democracia

Government

ARGENTINA
Mario Brodersohn
Minister of Finance

Juan Ciminari
Secretary of Communications

Francisco Delich
Secretary of Education

Horacio Juanarena
Minister of Defense

Marcelo Kiguel
Secretary of the Board of
  Government Industries

Roberto Lavagna
Minister of Industry

Jesús Rodriguez
Congressman

Federico Storani
Congressman

Marcelo Stubrin
Congressman

Pedro Trucco
Minister of Public Works and
  Services

DOMINICAN REPUBLIC
Eduardo Fernandez
Former President
Central Bank

Miguel Gerrero
Press Secretary to the President

Carlos Morales Troncoso
Vice President of the Republic

Pedro Morales Troncos
Former Director
Tourist Bureau

MEXICO
Luis Aguilera
Deputy Secretary
Department of Commerce and
  Industrial Development

Lucas de la Garza
Chief of Staff of the Governor's
  Office
Estado de Nuevo León

Miguel Mancera
General Director
Bank of México

Jorge Treviño
Governor
Estado de Nuevo León

PANAMA
Diómedes Concepción
Assistant Director General
National Port Authority

Dorothy de Sing
Vice-Minister
Ministry of Commerce and
   Industry

Miguel del Cid
Director of Planning
Ministry of Labor and Social
   Welfare

Rubén Darío Ortega Vieto
Deputy Executive Director
Instituto Panameño de Comercio
   Exterior

Juan Luis Moreno
Director
Office of Economic Planning
Ministry of Planning
   and Economic Policy

Rita Mariela Pérez
Adviser to the Minister
Ministry of Commerce and Industry

Julio Sosa
Executive Director
National Investment Council

Amílcar Villareal
Director
Nacional de Estadísticas

Labor

CHILE
Guillermo Medina
Union Representative
Corporación del Cobre
   (CODELCO)

Eduardo Ríos
Union Leader
Trabajadores Portuarios

Guillermo Santanta
Union Leader
Central Independiente de
   Trabajadores

MEXICO
Gustavo Flores Candanosa
General Coordinador
Federación Nacional de
   Sindicatos Independients

PANAMA
Ricardo Monterrey
Secretario General
Confederación de Trabajadores
   de la República de Panamá

PERU
Sixto Aguilar
Representative
Congreso Nacional del Perú

Mario Aranzaes
Secretary for Organization
Confederación Nacional de
   Trabajadores

Teófilo Carranza
Project Coordinator
Asociación Fomento de la Educación
   Laboral y Investigaciones
   Económicas y Sociales (AFELIES)

Julio Cruzado Zavala
President
Confederación de Trabajadores del
   Perú

Cástulo Fernández
Secretary of Organization
Federación de Trabajadores
 de Tejidos del Perú

Alex Kong Lu
Assistant
Asociación Fomento de la Ecucación
 Laboral y Investigaciones
 Económicas y Sociales (AFELIES)

Víctor Sánchez Zapata
President
Confederación Nacional de
 Trabajadores

Teodosio Torres
Secretary General
Confederación Nacional de
 Trabajadores

Political Analysis

ARGENTINA
Mariano Grondona
Television Commentator and
Editor, *A Fondo*

Luis Stulhman
Executive Director
Fundación para el Cambio en
 Democrácia

BRAZIL
Roberto Civita
Manager
Editora Abril, S.A.

Oliveiros S. Ferreira
Editor in Chief
O Estado de São Paulo

Eurico Figueiredo
Professor of Social Sciences
Federal University of Rio

Cándido Mendes de Almeida
Dean
Cándido Mendes University

Caio Tácito P. de Vasconcelos
Lawyer, Head of Presidential
 Commission to Create a Plan for
 the Reform of the Brazilian
 University System

CHILE
Pilar Armanet
Director
Instituto de Estudios Internacionales
University of Chile

Genaro Arriagada
Political Analyst

Carlos Cruz Coke
Lawyer

Gustavo Cuevas
Director
Institute of Political Science
University of Chile

Oscar Godoy
Director
Institute of Political Science
Catholic University

Francisco Orrego
Former Director
Institute of International Studies
University of Chile

MEXICO
José Luis Coindrau
Editorialist and Press Secretary
Partido Acción Nacional Eduardo
 Suárez

PANAMA
Laureano Crestar Durén, Pbro.
Parroquia Santísima Trinidad

Rubén Darlo Carles
President
La Prensa

Luis Shirley
Lawyer, Former Under Secretary
Ministery of Labor and Social
  Welfare

Appendix B   Americas Society Board of Directors and Chairman's Council Members participating in the study

Charles F. Barber	United States
R. P. Cezar de Andrade	Brazil
Gustavo Cisneros	Venezuela
John C. Duncan	United States
Henry Eder	Colombia
Agustín E. Edwards	Chile
José A. Estenssoro	Argentina
Jaime Garcia-Parra	Colombia
David Garza Laguera	Mexico
Marife Hernandez	United States
Amalia Lacroze de Fortabat	Argentina
George W. Landau	United States
Fernando Leniz	Chile
Allan MacEachen	Canada
John D. Macomber	United States
Jorge Mejía	Colombia
Seymour Milstein	United States
Martha Muse	United States
Arnaldo T. Musich	Argentina
Luis A. Noboa	Ecuador
Luisa E. M. de Pulido	Venezuela
David Rockefeller	United States
C. Fernando Romero	Bolivia
Julio Mario Santo Domingo	Colombia
Joaquín J. Vallarino	Panama
Paulo D. Villares	Brazil
Federico J. L. Zorraquin	Argentina

The views expressed in this report are not necessarily those of the participants in the study, listed above.

Other Publications from the Institute

POLICY ANALYSES IN INTERNATIONAL ECONOMICS SERIES

BOOKS

Economic Sanctions Reconsidered: History and Current Policy
Gary Clyde Hufbauer and Jeffrey J. Schott, assisted by Kimberly Ann Elliott/
1985

Trade Protection in the United States: 31 Case Studies
Gary Clyde Hufbauer, Diane T. Berliner, and Kimberly Ann Elliott/1986

SPECIAL REPORTS

1 **Promoting World Recovery: A Statement on Global Economic Strategy** *by
   Twenty-six Economists from Fourteen Countries/*December 1982

2 **Prospects for Adjustment in Argentina, Brazil, and Mexico: Responding to
   the Debt Crisis**
   *John Williamson, editor/*June 1983

3 **Inflation and Indexation: Argentina, Brazil, and Israel**
   *John Williamson, editor/*March 1985

4 **Global Economic Imbalances**
   *C. Fred Bergsten, editor/*March 1986

FORTHCOMING

The Politics of United States Trade Policy
(With The Twentieth Century Fund)
I.M. Destler

Agriculture and the GATT: Issues in a New Trade Round
Dale E. Hathaway

Another Multi-Fiber Arrangement?
William R. Cline

United States–Canadian Interdependence: The Quest for Freer Trade
Paul Wonnacott

Capital Flight and Third World Debt
Donald R. Lessard and John Williamson

Target Zones and Policy Coordination
Marcus Miller and John Williamson

The United States as a Debtor Country
C. Fred Bergsten and Shafiqul Islam

Domestic Adjustment and International Trade
Gary Clyde Hufbauer and Howard F. Rosen, editors

Auction Quotas and US Trade Policy
C. Fred Bergsten and Jeffrey J. Schott